The Gift of Dreams

The Gift of Dreams

Discover the power of the dream realm and your subconscious self

ROSE INSERRA

A Rockpool book
PO Box 252
Summer Hill
NSW 2130
Australia
www.rockpoolpublishing.com.au
www.facebook.com/RockpoolPublishing

ISBN 978-1-925017-83-0

First published in 2015 by Rockpool Publishing as
Dreams ISBN 978-1-925017-17-5.
This edition published in 2019

Design by Trenett Ha, Rockpool Publishing
Images by Shutterstock
Printed and bound in China

10 9 8 7 6 5 4 3 2 1

Contents

What You Need to Know About Dreams

'A dream is a microscope through which we look at the hidden occurrences in our soul.'
– Erich Fromm

Dreaming represents an important part of our lives – whether you remember your dreams or not, we do it every single night. It is a universal experience and more than just a biological function.

The ancient Egyptians were said to have written the oldest dream dictionary on papyrus, which dates back to 1250 BCE. Ancient Chinese visited temples and performed dream incubation, and understood the dream was therapeutic. Ancient India's book on wisdom, the Atharva Veda, contains many early beliefs about dream symbols. The Bible refers to dreams and interpretations. Native American Indians and the Indigenous peoples of Australia believe in the healing power of dreams and guidance obtained by a vision or vision quest.

Dreams, however, were not taken seriously in the Western world until psychologist Sigmund Freud (1856–1939) began to study them as part of psychoanalysis. He analysed and interpreted dreams as the place where unconscious fears, desires, sexual urges and repressions resided. For Freud, dreams were about the hidden parts of ourselves that we try to repress or reject. His work focused a great deal on finding the causes of dreams, using an analytical approach of free association in which the dreamer described thoughts and feelings as they came to mind.

In general, new theories suggest that dreams act as a safe place where we confront primal threats to our livelihood and survival. By confronting these fears in dreams, we rehearse how we deal with our waking-life challenges.

Our dreams can reveal many truths about our lives, giving us amazing insights that can provide information on health, relationships, work and our overall emotional state. Our subconscious is like a personal therapist. Understanding our dreams can bring self-awareness and a strong connection to our soul.

Sleep states

We all experience five stages or cycles of sleep each night, from the lightest sleep (stages 1-2) to the very deep sleep (stages 3-4) where it's difficult to wake someone up. Stage 5 sleep is known as REM sleep –the sleep period where we dream most vividly. During REM (rapid eye movement) sleep, when we dream, the brain is thought to be processing stored memory.

We sleep for about one third of our lives, and we have REM-sleep dreams for roughly one quarter of that time. It is estimated that we sleep for about twenty-five years and we dream for six of those years. In one year we have, on average, up to 1800 dreams of which we will only remember a few, if any.

Parts of the brain used in dreaming

Sleep studies show that dreams occur mostly in rapid eye movement (REM) cycles, but they can happen in other non-rapid eye movement (NREM) sleep phases as well, although they are not as vivid. This explains people being able to sleepwalk, which cannot happen in REM sleep because a person's muscles become temporarily paralysed – a phenomenon which takes place in the pons areas located in the brain stem and which travels upward through to certain sections of the brain.

How we see our dreams

People who become blind after birth can see images in their dreams, however if a person is born blind they may not be able to dream in images but their dreams are equally vivid. Other senses such as sound, touch, smell and emotions compensate for the lack of visionary stimulation.

Why We Dream

> *'The general function of dreams is to try and restore our psychological balance by producing dream material that re-establishes, in a subtle way, the total psychic equilibrium.'*
>
> *– Carl Jung*

There is plenty of evidence to support the mental and physiological benefits of dreams. We need to be aware of these benefits in order to understand how they relate to our present state of being.

Biological necessity

Our bodies need a specific amount of REM sleep to assist with recovery and repair. Sleep also restores functions such as memory and learning.

Dreaming, therefore, reduces stress and gives our busy, conscious mind a break while our brain and body regenerate.

To release, cleanse and process

Dreams help us get in touch with our emotions and bring imbalances to our attention. Our subconscious mind processes input from our everyday problems – stresses, anxieties, fears, self-doubt and repressed feelings – which can be filtered, sorted and then brought to the surface where healing can take place.

To investigate and problem solve

Dreams can help us pinpoint health problems, address major life issues, and help us to solve problems by shutting out the busy-ness of our waking brain and allowing our subconscious mind to explore solutions and possible scenarios without restrictions.

In preparation for future events

Dreams allow us to rehearse or practise for future events, as we dream up scenarios of potential real-life scenes. Nightmares help us prepare for possible traumatic events in our lives.

For creativity and inspiration

Dreams have had a huge impact on our inventions, creativity and inspiration. Recording artist Paul McCartney heard the tune of Yesterday in a dream. Author Stephen King dreamt the idea for his best-selling book Misery, as well as other characters and plots in his novels.

Spirituality

Dreams can be insightful and spiritually uplifting, as dreamers receive messages from their departed loved ones, spiritual guides or their own inner wisdom, and use these lessons in waking life.

Layers of Consciousness

Dreams are a biological necessity that keep us healthy by identifying patterns of behaviour, and releasing old and unhelpful belief systems and thoughts.

The Conscious

The conscious mind consists of all the mental processes of which we are aware. It gathers information from your five senses and makes all the decisions.

The Unconscious

According to Freud, the unconscious mind is described as being a reservoir of feelings, thoughts, urges and memories that are outside of our conscious awareness. Freud described the unconscious mind as an iceberg. Everything above the water represents conscious awareness, while everything below the water represents the unconscious. Somewhere in between the two is the subconscious.

The Subconscious

The subconscious, sometimes called the pre-conscious, can be defined as just outside of awareness but within our reach, while our unconscious is the deeper materials that haven't yet emerged into subconscious awareness – the rejected, forgotten, devalued or ignored parts of ourselves.

The Superconscious

The superconscious mind is not connected with our physical shell or body. It exists at a level beyond time and space. It is known as the Infinite Intelligence or the Universal Mind – one that we are all connected to. We can access this superconscious mind through spiritual dreams and precognitive or prophetic dreams.

Types of Dreams

Anxiety. Most dreams are anxiety based – that is, they highlight our waking-life anxieties that we mostly ignore or are not aware of.

Creative. Those working in creative fields such as art, music or literature are more directly impacted by creative dreams, which are a deep source of inspiration.

Compensatory. Whatever hasn't been given a healthy outlet or expression in your waking life has the potential to manifest as a negative, compensatory dream.

Wish-fulfilment. The purpose of a wish-fulfilment dream is not to show the dreamer what is missing in their life, but rather to show the potential that is in each of us to achieve our goals and dreams.

Precognitive. Dreaming of something before it happens (a future event) can be a confusing dream type as the dreamer has not much indication of whether it's a symbolic dream or a precognitive/prophetic dream until after the future event happens.

Warning. Warning dreams show us potential dangers that may pose a physical or psychological threat, especially if we have not heeded our intuition in our waking life.

Archetypal. An archetypal dream deals with a much bigger issue than simply a personal one. It deals with patterns of behaviour or belief systems that are universally shared.

Numinous. These 'big dreams' bring you in contact with the divine.

Shamanic. Dreams that involve elements of initiation, ritual, healing and guidance for the benefit of the dreamer and others (tribal) are manifested in distinct shamanic ways passed down from indigenous cultures and traditions.

Healing. A healing dream is one that heals your physical body, your emotional state and your relationships with others. It can offer you clues as to what illness you may have, even before medical diagnosis.

Para-psychological. Many dreams that cannot be explained logically fit into this dream type, such as telepathic dreams, dream sharing, afterlife, past lives, future or parallel lives.

Lucid/Astral Travel/Out-of-body experience (OBE). Lucid dreaming is 'knowing' or being aware that you are dreaming while you are dreaming. In some cases, you can control the events and outcome of the dream. Astral travel and OBE are being able to dream yourself out of your body and travel in the astral realm, often meeting other dreamers in these places.

What Dreams Tell You About Your Health

There are a number of symbols in your dreams that indicate illness or potential health problems. Having a mind-body connection means that all parts of our body and all of the emotional responses we have, share a common language and communicate with each other. When dreaming of any of these symbols, accidents or parts of the body, interpret them as being a message from your subconscious mind and take the images seriously. Illness can be detected by your body first, which then informs your psyche.

Symbol: House	Possible Meaning
Broken or blocked pipes	circulatory problems
Frozen or cold temperature	locked energy flow
Garbage	need to clean out/release, digestive problems
Renovation	healing needed, overhaul, change in diet
Burglary	open to infection, vulnerable
Flooding	excess, water retention, overwhelmed
Infestation	infection
Fire	fever, viral or bacterial infection, heartburn

Symbol: Illness	Possible Meaning
Allergies	be more tolerant of those around you
Cancer	something is eating away at you, part of your life is not being lived
Diarrhoea	allow yourself to be nurtured
Epilepsy	out of balance with life
Fever	anger, burning up with resentment
Infection	need to get rid of negative emotions, purify
Pneumonia	overwhelmed with emotions, inner turmoil
Rash	self-critical, unable to express yourself
Breathing problems/asthma	trying to please others, focus on what inspires you
Tumour	feeling unlovable, self-neglect
Vomiting	you can't stomach something, need to speak out and let go of old stuff

Symbol: Accidents	Possible Meaning
Burns	anger, soothe it with the balm of forgiveness
Cuts	emotional wounds
Run over or crushed	overwhelmed by stress or someone in your life, something is crushing your vision/spirit

Fall	lack of control, trust in yourself and the universe
Loss of limb	feeling disconnected or disempowered, time to take stock of a situation

Remembering Your Dreams

1. Take a sincere interest in your dreams. If you are interested in your dreams, there is a very high probability that you will remember them.
2. Set a clear intention throughout the day to remember a significant dream. You might want to re-read some of your previous dreams to start connecting to the subconscious imagery or alternatively meditate on a question you'd like answered. You may wish to write the question on paper and place it under your pillow.
3. The way you wake up is very important so that you don't forget your dreams. Within five minutes of waking, fifty per cent of your dream is forgotten. Within ten minutes, ninety per cent is gone. Set a soft alarm to wake you up fifteen to twenty minutes earlier than usual, when you are still in the REM dream state. Better still, avoid using an alarm clock and train your body to wake you instead.
4. When you wake, keep your eyes closed and remain completely still, focusing on the memory of the dream. Recall all the images, emotions

and scenes from your dream and jot them quickly in your dream journal.

5. Alcohol, caffeine, recreational drugs and medication diminish the ability to remember dreams, as does vitamin and mineral deficiency, particularly in the vitamin B group. Certain foods affect our dreams and therefore it's best to avoid heavy or spicy foods before bedtime when our bodies have not had time to digest. Interestingly, people who are giving up smoking have longer and more intense dreams – mostly about smoking – as a result of tobacco withdrawal.

Rest assured that your dreams will never give you more than you can handle. All that is bubbling away within your subconscious will only come up to the conscious when it is ready. There will be times when our emotional world needs release and recurring dreams and nightmares are a result of deep feelings and thoughts that we are conscious of. They bring to our attention those things we have repressed, that we perceive to be threatening, overwhelming or devastating at some point in our past. Carl Jung believed that it is our Shadow (rejected parts and qualities we do not like about ourselves) that usually appear as frightening nightmares in our dreams if we don't acknowledge them in our conscious state.

When Dreams are a Problem

'The unconscious always tries to produce an impossible situation in order to force the individual to bring out his very best. Otherwise one stops short of one's best, one is not complete, one does not realise oneself. What is needed is an impossible situation where one has to renounce one's own will and one's own wit and do nothing but wait and trust to the impersonal power of growth and development.'
– Carl Jung (on nightmares)

The point of the nightmare is a sign that you are now ready to deal with these emotions and unacceptable parts of your personality for the sake of your mental, physical and spiritual health. Believe it or not, your nightmare is there to help you. Night terrors happen in the cycle before REM sleep and usually have no visuals, although dreamers wake up screaming. The more typical nightmares are detailed and in colour. It is believed that up to twenty per cent of people have nightmares once a week.

Types of Recurring Dreams and Nightmares

There are many types of recurring dreams and nightmares that cause us fear, frustration, terror and sometimes physical pain. Some common negative dream scenarios include falling, being chased or attacked, being killed or killing someone, seeing someone you love die or in danger, late or unprepared for a presentation or an exam, stuck in slow motion, unable to move or scream, suffocation, sinister presence, to name a few. If we don't deal with issues highlighted in our nightmares, by blocking, ignoring or denying them, they may haunt us in other ways, manifesting as illnesses, accidents, conflicts in relationships and other personal difficulties. Nightmares are there to remind us of some urgent business to be resolved.

Resolving Nightmares

There are a number of methods you can use that will assist you in working with your nightmares so that you no longer dread them, but learn to harness the energy they offer. Insights from recurring dreams and nightmares can give you great confidence in expressing your feelings instead of avoiding or running away from situations that are unpleasant.

Some of the most useful techniques include dream re-scripting (changing the outcome of the dream once you learn to go back [dream re-entry] into the dream); and lucid dreaming (being awake in your dream and changing the events, such as asking the pursuer what they want or turning a potential weapon into a harmless object).

> *'I've dreamt in my life dreams that have stayed with me ever after, and changed my ideas: they've gone through and through me, like wine through water, and altered the colour of my mind.'*
>
> – Emily Bronte

Dreams can mean many things to each of us at any given time – they are a personal code and they are different for every individual. It is normal for dreams to be associated with events that happen during the day or with those repressed emotions buried deep within our unconscious.

Dreams are also connected to the intuition within our subconscious that is generally not heeded, and even to incidents that took place when we were children and have influenced us since in our attitudes and patterns of behaviour. Your highly intuitive and spiritual nature may be attuned to receiving important information about yourself and others while in the state of dreaming.

Understanding your dreams, therefore, is a powerful way to gain insight into your subconscious mind and bring dream messages into consciousness so that you can gain understanding and healing. This dream guide is simply that – a guide to help unlock symbols in your dreams that are meaningful to you personally and reflect your own inner world.

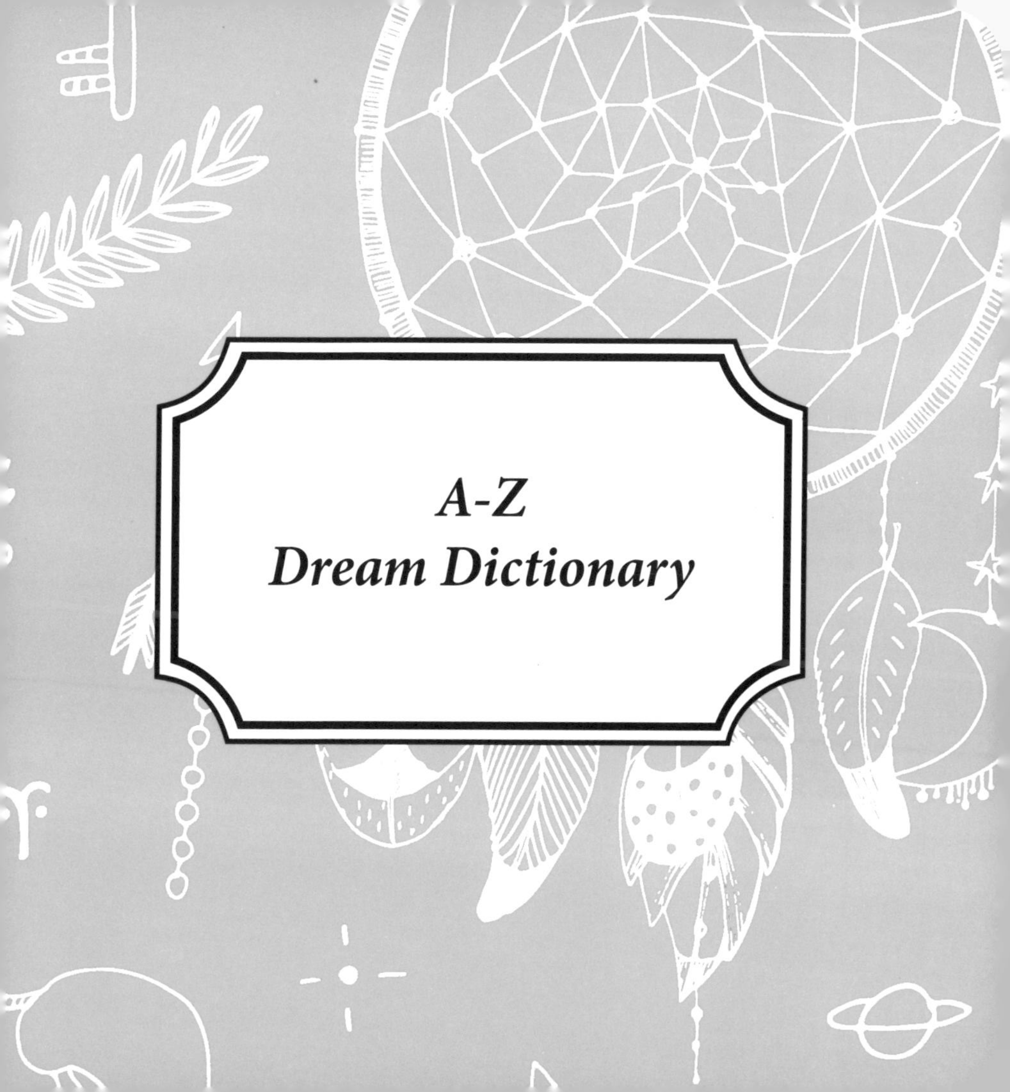

A-Z
Dream Dictionary

Accident see also Illness/Injury

Accidents bring attention to your safety and the importance of taking extra care of yourself in daily life. Are you feeling exhausted? Lacking in concentration and energy? Perhaps you have had some close calls – driving a little too far outside the lanes or brushing too close against a wall or door handle. Be aware and alert. Your body is telling you that you need to rest and concentrate. Is there an 'accident waiting to happen' on a physical or emotional level?

Angels

Throughout history, angels have been described as 'messengers' from a divine source. They represent goodness, protection and divine grace. To dream of angels is a good omen, forewarning you of some change in your situation. Their appearance could be a warning of things to come and to keep faith during trying times ahead.

Animals

Animals are believed to represent our own instinctual nature, habits and personality. To see domestic or pet animals in your dream, suggests you are familiar with those habits and behaviours that the animals represent.

Wild animals are more likely to represent the wild and unpredictable parts of our personalities. Each animal is unique to the dreamer's own relationship or association with that animal. For example, a dog can be considered a loyal companion, a disease carrier, an aggressive foe or even a menu item. When you dream of a dog, these perceptions will influence the message of the dream.

In indigenous cultures, animals are important totems and guides that carry a message and healing or 'medicine' components. Their meaning is quite different to the general understanding of meaning in dreams as symbols of our nature. When an animal totem or helper comes to us in dreams, their medicine will take time to integrate.

When you dream of animals, be aware of what that animal means to you and what characteristics you associate with it. Usually, it has to do with our instinctual drives. You unmask the personality trappings that make up your public and social persona, and are left with basic, deep, instinctual drives that are connected to the more natural world.

Helpless animals in need or rescue indicate parts of you that have been neglected or stored away for future use. Look at the specific animal in the dream to determine what parts of you need to be freed or given permission to do what they love (e.g. birds need to fly, dogs need loyalty and family).

In its positive aspect, the animal will give you insight about what needs to be worked on and changed in your life, and have access to deeper knowledge about your nature. In its negative aspect, the animal will make us aware of the threat we are dealing with in our own nature or in those around us. Hostile animals generally represent a person, problem or situation that is troubling you in real life. The dream shows you the threat and how to protect yourself so that on waking you can work out a strategy to deal with it.

Questions to ask yourself about the animal in your dream:

What qualities do I personally associate the animal with?

What qualities do I need to adopt/control?

What parts of me need to be nurtured?

What parts of me or those around me do I feel threatened by?

What is the message the animal brings me?

Here are some typical associations with common animals in our dreams, both positive and negative. I have included idioms that will bring up more associations for you and an overriding lesson or message to the dreamer based on the most commonly recognised characteristic of the animal in the dream.

Ants

Ants are commonly regarded as hard-working and resourceful. Their organisational skills, diligence and persistence are remarkable, and so in dreams they may represent these qualities that you take for granted or find monotonous. You may need to continue to work hard and consistently to achieve your goal. Teamwork and asking for help are also key factors to your success. If the ants were annoying in your dream, it could be time for you to change or sort out your lifestyle, habits or work.

Idioms: ants in your pants, antsy, working (hard) like ants

Lesson: Patience/teamwork

Birds

Birds have always been connected to flight and therefore associated with freedom. Traditionally they are thought to bring messages through their song and sound, as well as their vantage point from high above. They are often interpreted as the symbol of our soul's longing and aspirations. A bird that is injured or unable to fly suggests that some area of your life needs attending to before you will be able to 'move on'.

Idioms: a little bird told me, free as a bird, bird's-eye view, the birds and the bees, the early bird catches the worm, the bird has flown, eagle eyes, nest egg, feather one's nest, hawk (ruthless person or offer of sales in street), watch someone like a hawk, sitting duck, lame duck, chicken feed, as wise as an owl

Lesson: Perception/freedom

There are many types of birds with individual associations. Here are the most common species:

Eagles are the most majestic of birds, representing power, authority, perfect hunting skills and precision. The eagle is considered a highly spiritual animal in shamanic traditions. Are you making wise and strategic choices?

Owls appear as symbols of an ending or at the passing of a loved one. They represent wisdom and intuition or psychic abilities.

Ravens and crows are symbols of the mystical side of life. They appear at endings, new beginnings and denote spiritual progress to come.

Water birds such as herons, cranes, ducks and swans connect with our emotional and subconscious nature.

Bull

As an astrological sign, Taurus, the bull, represents determination, passion and strength. Are these qualities you need in your real life? Do you need to be more grounded and pragmatic? On the negative aspect, if you fight or flee from a bull, it may symbolise negative, destructive and impulsive emotions you may be experiencing.

Idioms: like a bull at a gate, like a bull in a china shop, take the bull by the horns, bully

Lesson: Determination

Cats

Cats represent our feminine nature with their refined qualities of independence, intuition and sleek appearance. Their hunting skills make them powerful predators and this duality makes them an interesting domestic companion – making people often wary and distrustful of them. Ancient Egyptians worshipped cats and the Romans even considered them household gods. Black cats were once regarded as evil, treacherous and the witches' familiars. If you dream of cats, be aware of what qualities you admire/dislike in a cat and whether the dream is asking you to adopt some of its characteristics.

Idioms: catty, play cat and mouse, cat calls, copycat, catnap, let the cat out of the bag, curiosity killed the cat, a cat on a hot tin roof, raining cats and dogs, like cat and dog, when the cat's away, the mice will play

Lesson: Independence

Dogs

Dogs have been domesticated mostly for companionship and for their assistance in hunting, guarding, defending and working. They can be loyal and devoted companions or in some cultures are considered dirty scavengers. If you are a dog lover, your dreams will make associations with all the positive aspects of dogs. Are these qualities what you want to see more of in your own nature? Are you being a good friend? Are your friendships in need of a review? If you dream of a dog biting you, it may represent your aggressive traits or of those around you. It may all be a loud bark with no bite, so look carefully at the situation.

Idioms: top dog, underdog, dog tired, a dog's breakfast, a dog's life, dog eat dog, cat and dog, let sleeping dogs lie, can't teach an old dog new tricks

Lesson: Loyalty

Dolphins

Dolphins were once regarded as sacred. Their intelligence, compassion, friendliness and intuition are commonly admired. When dreaming of dolphins, you are accessing your deepest intuitions and creativity, but you must release your emotional blockages and tension first.

Idioms: playful dolphins, dolphin pod

Lesson: Communication

Elephants

Elephants are the largest land mammals and we make the obvious associations with their sheer size and strength. In dreams we can't help but notice them. They represent memory and family ties, reminding us of who we're meant to be and what we are doing to stay on track. Their wisdom and patience are what makes these graceful creatures symbols of good luck and prosperity in some cultures.

Idioms: a white elephant, a memory like an elephant, big enough to shade an elephant, jumbo size, elephantine

Lesson: Think big/knowledge

Fish

Fish are associated with good luck and prosperity in Eastern cultures. The astrological symbol of the fish is also the Pisces, whose many qualities include creativity and self-expression. Dreaming of fish suggests we are getting in touch with our deeper emotional selves. Look at your emotional life and be gentle on yourself if you feel out of your depth, a fish out of water (not belonging), or living in a fishbowl (feeling criticised). What/who are you fishing (searching) for and are you using the right bait or lure to catch them?

Idioms: fishing for a compliment, a different kettle of fish, bigger fish to fry, drink like a fish, big fish in a small pond

Lesson: Self-awareness

Frogs

Frogs are a symbol of transformation due to their metamorphosis from their tadpole state – changing from something small to something of greater value, such as the frog turning into a prince. They are known as our ecological barometer – alerting us when waters and the environment are polluted. When you see frogs in your dream consider if you require some form of cleansing and what you need to clear out to be able to breathe more freely.

Idioms: frog in your throat, fine as frog hair, raining frogs, ugly as a toad

Lesson: Renewal/transformation

Lions

Lions are the classic kings of the jungle and symbols of ego, power, majesty, strength and courage. If you see a lion in your dreams, it may suggest that you may need to assert your authority and let yourself be heard (roar). If you run from a lion, you may be feeling lacking in courage in your waking life. Surviving a lion attack indicates you will overcome a struggle. Does the lion represent you or someone else in your life? Take care to put your power and ego to good use. It may also stand for the astrological sign of Leo.

Idioms: as strong as a lion, a lion's share, lionhearted, into the lion's den

Lesson: Courage

Monkeys

Monkeys are the cheeky and playful aspects of our nature. They are considered clever and wise – the three monkeys of see no evil, hear no evil, speak no evil. The dream may be telling you to clown around more and enjoy having fun in social occasions or simply be more quick-witted when it's required. A monkey on your back is about problems that won't let go and you may need to learn to discern and sort out what's really important.

Idioms: monkey see, monkey do, make a monkey of, monkey suit, monkey's uncle, monkey business, a barrel of monkeys

Lesson: Curiosity/humour

Rabbits

Rabbits are recognised as symbols of fertility and new life, with the Christian Easter celebrations and commercialisation keeping this traditional meaning alive in our psyche. Like hares, rabbits are quick and nimble. Your dream may suggest that you will be coming across new ventures; however, it's important that you pace yourself and stay on course to avoid burn-out.

Idioms: quick as a rabbit, breed like rabbits, pull a rabbit out of a hat, bunny

Lesson: Self-control/new growth

Snakes

Snakes have in the past been associated with deceit, trickery, sexual urges and danger. We are all aware that snakes can pose a danger to one's life and by making this connection at a subconscious level, we dream of snakes as being warning symbols. Is it a warning from areas of your life that need to be protected? A snake in your dream will certainly alert you to potential threats that are lurking in your waking life, and it may pay you to remain vigilant when your intuition reinforces the dream's images.

Snakes in dreams have also been regarded in high esteem for their healing properties, wisdom, life-and-death cycle and transformation. Symbolically, snakes could represent a hidden threat, as in 'snake in the grass'. A snake shedding its skin may be a symbol of renewal, in which case a snake dream could be seen as a positive omen. What old life are you shedding in favour of a new skin that is more appropriate to your growth?

The alchemical symbol of the snake swallowing or eating its own tail is known as the ouroboros. An ouroboros dream, therefore, may indicate a time of change and transformation for the dreamer. The ouroboros represents the perpetual cyclic renewal of life and infinity, eternity, the cycle of life, death and rebirth.

In Kundalini yoga, the snake is the energy centre coiled at the base of your spine. This is the place of creativity and instincts and you may gain insight into your deepest inner knowing. Chinese astrologers consider those born under the sign of the snake as having great wisdom, sensuality and diplomacy, and the snake year is usually one that brings about significant changes.

The staff of Asklepios, the ancient Greek healer, had serpents entwined about it, and the symbol of the medical field itself (the staff with two serpents) is a reference to the healing power of snakes and Asklepios' medical practice.

Other symbols associated with the snake are the male sexual energy (phallic symbol) or your own sexuality. You may need to be more comfortable with this part of yourself. A snake in your dream may be a symbol of an ancient, forgotten wisdom that has been replaced by modern beliefs. Being attacked, threatened or finding yourself in a snake pit suggests basic underlying fears of danger and death. Your personal association with snakes is what will give you a clearer understanding of your dream.

Idioms: a snake in the grass, mad as a cut snake, lower than a snake's belly, snake oil, snake along, snake eyes, snake pit, snaky

Lesson: Healing/wisdom

Spiders

Generally, spiders weave intricate webs to catch unsuspecting prey, and dreaming about spiders may indicate you feel that you are being manipulated or drawn into a web of intrigue or suspicion. If you are genuinely afraid of spiders, dreaming of them is a projection of your fears, which is possibly triggered by something that is making you scared in real life. Are there conflicts going on around you that you can't control?

Traditionally spiders are connected with creativity as weavers of webs (Arachne in ancient Greek myth was a master weaver and we have the word arachnids from the language), and also with powerful female and mother figures. The Spider Woman, sometimes referred to as The Spider Grandmother, is portrayed in Native American myth as the Mother who created all life. She is represented as the woman who sits in the middle of the universe spinning her web, connecting all living beings to each other.

The dream is encouraging you to search your heart and reconnect with your own creativity and then share that with others.

Idioms: blow away the cobwebs, web of life, tangled web, spidery veins

Lesson: Connection/creativity

Wolves

Wolves have been maligned and misunderstood in European societies in the past. Indigenous peoples called the wolf 'brother' due to the profound teachings it gave humans. Powerful and highly intelligent wolves are social creatures and cooperate in packs for the sake of the group, however, they can be solitary too. If you dream of a wolf, it may be telling you to find freedom, passion and return to your authentic self. The wolf may represent people in your life or parts of yourself who threaten you, make you feel vulnerable and seem beyond your control. The dream is telling you to trust your inner voice.

Idioms: keep the wolf from the door, lone wolf, throw to the wolves, to wolf down, a wolf in sheep's clothing, to cry wolf

Lesson: Knowledge

Anger

When dreams are compensatory it means that we don't express our true feelings openly in real life because of the perceived potential consequences, and those emotions which cannot be contained come out in our dreams. Are you feeling anger and afraid to express it? Perhaps you may not be aware that you are feeling this way.

Army

An army is associated with discipline and obedience. Where do these qualities sit in your life? Is your life a battle? How do you simply 'soldier on' in the face of obstacles?

Attacked

If you are attacked in dreams it may reflect those same feelings of being attacked emotionally in your life. Who is attacking you? Identifying the attacker may give you an indication of what's causing you to feel threatened emotionally or even physically.

B

Babies/Birth/Child see also Pregnancy

Babies in dreams represent the creation of something new – a new phase in life, a new relationship, a new project or a new beginning. A helpless, abandoned, crying baby, or even a small animal, indicates that you've neglected or put on hold a creative project or a relationship that needs your attention. Are you nurturing your inner child with some fun and spontaneity? If it's a new career, a lifestyle change, or a new creative project, make sure you protect and nurture them so that they can 'grow' into whatever it is that you envisioned.

A forgotten baby indicates that something you began long ago has been put on hold and the dream is jolting your memory to renew your interest. It can also suggest that you are overloaded and need to prioritise so that you don't neglect those areas in life that you care about. If the baby is ill or distressed you may be feeling overwhelmed by responsibility and unable to nurture and commit to something or someone. It may represent those underdeveloped parts of you that need parenting. Death during childbirth represents a transformation of one thing ending and a new one beginning. There are changes and transitions occurring in your life.

Balloon

Balloons are associated with celebrations and good times. They could indicate you are longing for a change of scenery.

Bathroom see also Toilet and House

Bathing is a symbol of purification, regeneration and preparation for a new day. Water is also a symbol of our emotions; so, if you dream of having a bath, it may be a sign that you are washing away feelings or detoxifying.

A typical anxiety dream is looking for a bathroom/toilet, being unable to find it or it's broken or, worse, in public view. If you need to use the bathroom to relieve yourself but can't find it, are you allowing yourself the basic needs of life? You may need more private space and time to do what you need to do.

If the toilet's blocked/broken/overflowing you may need to release something in your life that has served its purpose and it's time to let go of it. Ask yourself what's blocked in your life. What sort of 'wastes' in my life are overflowing around me, affecting my quality of life? What basic needs am I depriving myself of and what negative emotions do I need to release and relieve myself of? Is there an element of shame in this? Sometimes dreaming about toilets is your body's message that you need to wake up and use the bathroom.

Being exposed to the public while using the toilet suggests that you are feeling vulnerable in your real life and not happy about sharing your personal life in public. However, sometimes it's a good idea to share some of our burdens with others and learn to cope with vulnerability in order to form close friendships.

Bed/Bedroom see also House

Beds are a representation of rest, of dreaming, comfort, security and intimacy. The condition of the bed is relevant – is it clean? Is it inviting? Is your life a bed of roses or on the negative side, have you made your own bed and now you must lie in it?

Bicycle

A bicycle is a visual representation of how you are progressing and travelling in life – look at how easy your ride is. If it's bumpy or you fall off, get ready for some challenges ahead.

Boat see also Vehicles and Water

A boat symbolises our hopes and fears, as this mode of transport carries us over water (our emotional life). If the water is calm, you feel reassured that all is going as it should, but storms and fear of capsizing are an indication that you are not in control and anxieties or fears could potentially overwhelm you. Hold your ground during an emotional conflict storm. If you miss the boat, it suggests you are not feeling prepared for a new opportunity or relationship.

Body see also Colours – Chakras

The human body is made up of many different parts, and one or more of these may be prominent in a dream. If a particular part of the body is vivid in your dreams, your subconscious is trying to bring your attention to that region. What parts of you do you need to examine more closely? What's not functioning in your life? Do you have a healthy sense of self-esteem? The body dream may also be alerting you to a potential health problem, so make sure you follow up with medical advice if the dream is worrying you and you are experiencing new symptoms.

Arms

Arms suggest embracing all that life brings on a metaphysical level. What are you striving for? Are you being nurturing or nurtured in relationships?

If you dream of an arm being amputated you may be anxious about losing someone significant to you (losing my right arm).

Dismembered/loss of limb

Being dismembered or losing a limb suggests that you are feeling fragmented and not connected to those parts of yourself in the dream. If your arms have been cut, think about what you are not 'handling' well or are unable to embrace and accept. What have I been neglecting, or forgetting? (Dismembering is the opposite of remembering.)

Faeces

Faeces is a natural bodily function, representing that which we need to release or expel from our system and clean up. It may disgust you to see faeces in your dream, but remember that it is also a great fertiliser. What aspects of yourself do you need to grow?

Genitals see also Sex

Genitals in your dreams represent your personal feelings towards sex, sexuality, the feminine and masculine roles, and your attitude to commitment, expression and pleasure. Loss of genitals indicates fears or lack of sexual confidence and inadequacy. Having genitals of the opposite sex suggests your need for balance (yin and yang; Anima and Animus).

Hair

Hair has long been associated with our sexual attractiveness and strength (think of the biblical hero Samson). Wild, tangled hair can symbolise self-critical thoughts. Long, seductive hair suggests the desire for sexual fulfilment. If you have knots in your hair, you may need to untangle your real-life problems.

Head

Head relates as much to the intellect as it does to your overall personality, aspirations and fears. A disembodied head signifies imbalance in your life. If you dream of something happening to your brain it represents that something in your life is affecting your perspective and judgement. How do you process information? A change of thinking is represented by brain surgery.

Legs and feet

Legs and feet represent our support – our foundation in life. Legs carry us forward into new situations and places. They are our 'drive' and what motivates us. We simply need the right shoes to be comfortable with our identity and life path. If you dream of not being able to move your legs, perhaps you've lost your confidence or have experienced a broken relationship and are trying to adapt to a new status.

Teeth

Teeth are traditionally associated with aggression, vulnerability, ageing and self-expression. Dreams of broken or missing teeth suggest you are feeling vulnerable, unattractive and powerless – that you have little or no control over your life. You may fear that you are losing your voice (metaphorically speaking) or have problems with verbalising what you think.

Bomb

You may be feeling explosive inside, keeping your emotions in check or facing an explosive situation. An unexpected event could blow up after a long brewing of deep feelings.

Bridge

Crossing a bridge suggests movement from one state to another, which can be dangerous because you are leaving known territory, and exciting too because you don't know what's on the other side. When two sides are unwilling to compromise, we talk about needing to build a bridge to meet halfway. 'Water under the bridge' is to let go of old hurts, and 'cross the bridge when you come to it' means to not act until it's the right time. How you feel in the dream is the key to your emotional landscape.

Generally, this dream is asking you to make some decisions during a time of potential transitions.

Buildings

Buildings represent the way we feel about our inner environment. What's the current status of your emotional, mental and physical health? Buildings associated with business remind us of our progress, or lack of, in our working life, career and social status. Is the building on solid foundations? How do you fit into the scene? What condition is the building in? All of these highlight the many aspects of your dreams and affect the overall meaning.

Castle

You may be wanting a space where you can be protected and defended against threatening people or situations. Is your home your castle? Is it a sanctuary or is it a place to keep others away?

Church/temple

Sacred or religious buildings offer us respite and help us to reflect on our spiritual lives, our values and ethics. You may be experiencing a desire to develop your spiritual life more fully or need some respite from the outside world.

Hotel

Hotel rooms suggest a temporary stay for work, travel or holidays and may indicate your wish for a change in these areas of your life.

Burglar

If you are being burgled in your dreams, it may reflect your real-life fears of someone intruding on your privacy and taking something away from you. Home, relationships and work areas need to be examined if you are fearful in your dreams.

Buried Alive

This terrifying dream is in the same category as being trapped or imprisoned. Take it as a positive indication that others are ignoring your needs and don't take on any more commitments.

Bus

If you are driving the bus, you are carrying a load of responsibilities but you are also in control. Ask yourself if this is satisfying you. If you are on the wrong bus you are conflicted as to the choices you make and what others expect of you. Missing a bus indicates your real-life feeling that you are missing out on something. Waiting for the bus suggests you are frustrated with the time it's taking to achieve your goals or take up opportunities.

C

Car

A car is a typical image of the self – your drive and ambition – and the direction your life is going. Ask yourself how you are travelling in life and if you're driving in the right direction of your goals.

Caves

Caves represent a sanctuary we can retreat into so that we can rest and regain our mental/physical strength. It is also a symbol of the unconscious, exploring our deepest darkest emotions that are kept hidden from the conscious. The cave is the archetypal place of initiation where you remain until you are ready to emerge as a newer version of you.

Chased

Being chased represents your real-life feelings of insecurity and powerlessness. What circumstances do you need to get away from? Take note of who's chasing you. What qualities does that person have to make you feel vulnerable? What aspect of yourself is causing you anxiety?

Child see also Babies

Children are symbols of those things that we value or we feel a great sense of responsibility for. If the child is happy, it indicates your sense of harmony and competence; if crying, you may need to find what's making you feel uncomfortable about a situation.

Clock

Traditional clocks have been replaced with digital displays that come with appliances, mobile phones, computers and more. It's the 'time' factor that reminds us that time is ticking away. Do you need to wake up to something? Finish a job or commit to a personal goal? Check your appointment times, too, as we tend to have this dream when we feel we may miss or be late for an appointment.

Colours

Most of us dream in colour, but as the dream fades upon waking, so do the colours and therefore we sometimes assume that we've dreamt in black and white. Colour in dreams is very significant, especially when the symbol is vivid or unusually coloured. A pink elephant, a blue wedding dress or a green sky is our mind's way of bringing these colours to our attention for a reason. Colours carry positive or negative meanings depending on our emotional, physical and mental state. You may be afraid to admit to having certain feelings about situations in your life or you may not be consciously aware of your emotions. The palette is a reflection of our inner landscape.

It is important to note that dreams can mean so many things to each individual at any given time and could even mean more than one thing within the same dream. These common colours are typically associated with the following images and feelings.

It is said that we have seven main energy centres, called chakras that are associated with specific colours and are connected to major organs or glands that rule other body parts. If there is an imbalance or blockage on any level – physical, emotional, mental and spiritual – we will be out of sync and our vitality will be affected. When dreaming of colours, it may be your chakras that need alignment or unblocking.

Red

Red evokes feelings of anger, danger, aggression, passion, power and energy. It is typically associated with blood and therefore the dream is showing you life energy – loss of blood equals death. Are you feeling depleted of energy? Is your health in good shape? To see red in dreams can mean that you are feeling angry and out of control, or it's a warning. You may turn red with embarrassment (shame) or be unable to control your sexual impulses. We are made aware that red lingerie is 'hot' and sexy, and the 'red light district' is strictly a place for prostitution.

1st Chakra: Red – Manifestation

Location: Root chakra at the base of the spine; coccyx.

If you are feeling unsettled, you may dream in red images, or have pain in the spine and lower back. Red symbolises the earth, and grounding yourself using your survival instincts is a good way to honour the dream.

Message Your life stability is in a state of transition.

Orange

Orange is the colour of warmth, friendship, kindness, self-respect and positive symbols associated with the sun, the warm glow of the fire, a new dawn or sunset. It gives us a sense of vitality and optimism, and therefore is centred on connecting to our senses and our creativity. Seeing orange in your dreams can also point to difficulty in being social or having intimacy issues.

2nd Chakra: Orange – Creativity

Location: Below navel, lower abdomen, sacral, genitals

If you are having dreams with orange colours, you may be dealing with fears relating to the areas of this chakra.

Message Get creative in new ways so that you don't do the same old thing. Find a new way to express yourself.

Yellow

Yellow is considered a happy colour, symbolising harmony, good mood, energy, awareness and mental stimulation. We connect yellow with the sun, and to have a sunny outlook on life means we are feeling positive. A coward is someone who is yellow and the colour is also associated with deceit, betrayal and sickness. How you feel in the dream holds the clue to its message.

3rd Chakra: Yellow – Empowerment

Location: Above the navel, stomach, solar plexus

Yellow is the colour of fire and the place where we feel purpose and power of transformation. This is where we start to put our changes into action and move forward. The dreams that occur here are dreams of struggle within ourselves. You may dream of yellow images and dream that you feel ill, especially in the stomach area.

Message Have faith in yourself, but also in your higher self.

Green

Green is normally associated 'newness' – someone is green when they are inexperienced. It's also the colour we connect to nature, the environment, good health, growth and healing. Turning green may also be associated with mould and decay, envy, insecurity and greed – so it's essential that you are aware of this duality. Have you had new ideas or directions that are now sprouting into life? Are you beginning a new project or phase?

4th Chakra: Green – Love

Location: Centre of chest, heart

This chakra is associated with love, compassion and healing. It is the central point of the chakra system – the centre of love. It is about our connectedness to all and our ability to love. Our dreams can be filled with many different things at this point because we are tested at our ability to truly love. If you dream in green images or colour, you may have a strong drive to help others, but beware of burn-out.

Message There are times where you need to lead with your heart rather than your head.

Blue

Blue is commonly recognised as the colour for truth, heaven, sky, sea, peace, intuition, and is therefore a spiritual colour. It is associated with boys and the masculine, and different shades of blue are generally favoured for uniforms. Feeling blue is a negative association with the colour, suggesting depression and sadness. If you dream of someone wearing blue, they may have something to communicate that is truthful and spiritual.

5th Chakra: Blue – Truth

Location: Throat

Express yourself through sounds, tones and chants. This chakra is associated with communication, thinking and planning. You may experience dreams in bright blue images or have a sore throat and be unable to speak. It may be that you lose your voice or choke.

Message Sing, chant, make sounds or create music. Make it up, be creative with it, and express your depths via non-verbalised/structured form.

Purple

Purple contains the tones of indigo (6th chakra) and violet (7th chakra) and often represents compassion, healing and kindness. In history, it was considered a royal colour, and those in high rank and priests were able to wear the rich colour of purple. If you dream of this colour you may be aiming to succeed at your work or be in search of validation.

Deep purple is associated with mystery and a new sense of self-awareness through intuition. Violet has a more spiritual meaning and is connected with spirituality or to a Higher power.

6th Chakra: Indigo – Vision

Location: Third eye, forehead

The sixth chakra is associated with intuition, seeing beyond the physical and psychic insight.

Message Envision your desired future joy.

7th Chakra: Violet – Transformation

Location: Crown, top of head

The seventh chakra is associated with our link to a higher spiritual realm or to Source/God, which connects us to the divine. It is considered as thought, knowing, understanding and transcendence. When this chakra is active, the violet turns to white, which is the ultimate spiritual shade.

Message You have permission to shine.

Black

Black is not an actual colour. It's a shade or the absence of light, and it symbolises the unknown, the unconscious and the deeper side of yourself. It is synonymous with 'black' and 'shadow' and therefore it may represent an idea, a person, a state of your life or your negative emotions, such as danger, emptiness, death, mourning, despair, depression, fatigue and lack of love. It may simply be that you are hiding something – those rejected or unacceptable aspects of yourself known as the Shadow. On a positive side, seeing black or dreaming in black and white may be pointing you to new directions or to hidden, unexplored potential. Is there anything lacking warmth of colour (variety) in your life?

Message What needs to be brought out of the darkness and into the light?

White

White is also a shade and not a colour. It is generally associated with purity, enlightenment, joy, religious figures, spirituality and spirit guides. We use white to symbolise new beginnings in rituals such as christenings and weddings. In cultures where white is worn at funerals, death is regarded as a new beginning or a transition rather than an ending. However, if you dream of white and if you feel it has more of an eerie feeling to it, it may refer to blinding white or bareness where nothing happens. To cover up what embarrasses us is also referred to as 'white out' or 'white wash'.

Message Is it time for you to become more aware and 'see the light'?

Court

Are you anxious of being judged? Do you have a guilty conscience or a need to claim justice? Dreaming of being in court suggests that you may be feeling that you are not being fairly treated (or your situation) and you are seeking retribution or compensation.

Crying

Crying often expresses sadness and hurt, and in dreams indicates that the dreamer has not released some unvented emotion in real life. It may also suggest that their needs are not being attended to.

D

Danger

Dreams exaggerate impending danger, whether it's a natural or manmade disaster or simply finding yourself in a dangerous situation. This is a reflection of how you see your life at the moment – filled with insecurity and potential threats. If you feel responsible for saving others, it highlights your personal heroic qualities.

Death/Dead

Death dreams are among the most universal common dreams. Unless someone you know is dying or very unwell, dreaming of death is an ending of something and a beginning of something new. As ancient philosopher and poet Lao Tzu tells us, 'New beginnings are often disguised as painful endings.'

Directions

Directions are important symbols in your dreams. Forward or in front represents the future (forward in time), while backward or behind is often a symbol of the past. Up or high indicates a spiritual or intellectual approach to life and downward is about being more instinctive and grounded. On the right indicates logic and reasoning, and to the left are emotional and artistic tendencies. Dark/underground is a symbol of the unconscious/subconscious and light/above ground is our consciousness.

Divorce

Dreaming of being divorced or separated may reflect your concerns about your relationships – not necessarily to do with your partner. Is it time to reassess your relationships? The dream suggests that a split or some distance away from a person, situation or an emotion may be necessary if it is no longer beneficial to your wellbeing. Losing money or lifestyle is also a major anxiety that may be manifested as a divorce dream.

E

Earthquakes

Earthquakes are the opposite of solid ground and represent emotional upheaval. Perhaps this eruption of emotions may enable you to make major changes from which you can grow, such as career changes, loss of job, selling up and moving away, divorce, retirement or unexpected events where your life's foundations are shattered. Sometimes this dream may be a precognitive dream if you are a highly intuitive person.

Eating see also Food

Eating in dreams suggests that you feel satisfied and your needs are being met. Sharing food represents you sharing yourself with others. There are many idioms connected with food – eat your words, dog eat dog, eat dirt, eaten out of house and home – and all have an association with consuming. Are there negative emotions that consume you? What type of nourishment do you need for your body, soul and mind?

EGG see also Food

Eggs are symbols of potential new life. Perhaps it may be your own potential or that of a new venture, project, life change or phase that has not yet been realised.

ELEVATORS/LIFTS

Elevators or lifts reflect how well we are progressing with a problem or current issue in our waking life. The movement of the lift and malfunctions reflect your attitudes and actions, which are either helping you to move towards your goals and aspirations or pulling you off track. Dreaming of a lift that crashes downward or flips you upwards occurs when there are major changes in your real-life role – it may be the added responsibility that creates an imbalance between what you thought was ideal and reality. A lift going up is connecting with our intellectual and rational side; going down is reaching into our subconscious mind for some answers.

F

Falling

Are you feeling unsupported in your waking life? Perhaps a situation has you feeling out of control at work or at home.

Fire

Fire is a symbol of urgency, passion and transition. What's urgent in your life right now? Are you feeling 'under fire'? Fire also purifies and therefore cleanses by burning, turning the original material into ashes. In this sense, fire is transformative and represents transition – from base to consumable; from the ashes there is new life and growth. If you dream of being on fire or your child being on fire, consider whether you are going through a transition period – it may be physical changes such as into adolescence or menopause. Other changes can include relationships, moving location, death of a loved one and anything that requires an element of transformation.

Is there a fire that burns within you? It may be that your fire represents a smouldering passion that you'd like to put into action. If the fire is burning out of control, it suggests that you are struggling to control your emotions (all fired up). Fire can destroy and create something new, so ask yourself whether there is an opportunity for regrowth. Be careful not to suffer burn-out, as fires can rage and then burn out quickly.

Flowers see also Garden

Flowers are an expression of beauty, perfection and joy. When we give and receive flowers it's an exchange of gratitude, love and appreciation. Note whether you are giving or receiving flowers, as this may indicate your desire for appreciation, respect, approval or admiration.

Blooming flowers represent your hidden potential and becoming more self-aware about your place in the world. Are you a late bloomer? Perhaps a new relationship is about to bloom – with yourself or with others. Faded or wilting flowers suggest the passing of a season or a phase (cycle) or time in our lives that is coming to an end. Life, like flowers, is about transitions, cycles and fragility. Is your life coming up roses? Is it a bed of roses? These idioms suggest the way in which society identifies flowers with lifestyle.

Look at the colour, condition and species of the flowers in your dream to gain greater insight into their presence. There are traditional symbolic meanings of flowers that may assist you in understanding the general association with that individual flower. For example, rose meanings vary according to colour but generally they are a symbol of deep love, balance, passion and intelligence. They can be a message for healing and courage. Only the dreamer can define their own association with the flower.

Food

Food is a symbol of our basic needs for physical, mental and emotional nourishment. Its function is to keep us alive and healthy, and to bring enjoyment. In any area of your life where this is lacking, your dream will bring it to your attention. Preparing healthy food suggests that you'd like a more balanced lifestyle. Cooking is all about being creative in the kitchen – the hearth of the home – and this applies to your personal and working life.

We use food to celebrate social occasions and important events – it connects us to others and creates bonds in relationships. A party or celebration represents your search for new ideas, perspectives and social attitudes. If the food is spoilt or indigestible, it denotes that there is a principle that you cannot 'swallow' or be part of. Choking and vomiting food is another type of aversion.

Look at what each food type represents in areas of your life that are associated with basic needs – bread, for example, is a staple food we need for survival and it's also slang for money, as is dough. Some common idioms about food – brain food, fast food, food for thought, junk food, mood food – can assist in highlighting your association with food in the dream.

What needs nourishment in real life? Are you lacking or feeling deprived in any areas of your life? What will make you feel abundant? What 'feeds' you, your soul, your ideas or your life in general?

Furniture

Furniture services our needs with its functionality, so we use tables and chairs for meals, sofas for relaxing, beds for sleeping and intimacy, and so on. In dreams, furniture is a symbol of our attitudes and values, depending on the outcome of the dream. A wardrobe or cupboard stores hidden memories and experiences; a bare or broken table may suggest your feelings of not having an active social or family life. Examine the association you make with the furniture piece and its function, and relate it to your experiences and attitudes.

G

Games/sport

Games represent the way you interact with social structures, playing the game of life, using strategies and training to work out how to survive and succeed. Solitary games suggest your preference for self-direction, while an interactive game highlights your inclination for competition and challenge.

Various games reflect the ways you navigate through life at a social level. Card games indicate risk and luck, while chess is a game of strategy and patience. Your dream game will give you clues regarding what you feel comfortable playing. It may be telling you that it's time to change the game or go up a level in order to make progress. Conversely the dream may be alerting you to have more fun. Perhaps your psyche is reminding you that it's not whether you win or lose but how you play the game that counts.

Gardens see also Flowers

A garden represents your inner landscape. A lush and well-kept garden is an indication that you are both creative and organised, whereas an untidy or abandoned garden suggests that you are lacking in order, focus, direction and perhaps not dealing with past hurts or disappointments. What needs weeding in your garden?

Gates

Walking through a gate is a sign of a new venture or new path in your waking life. Opening your gate represents allowing things to be possible as you are open to them, but be careful not to 'open the floodgates' as this may contain emotions that overwhelm you. If your gate is closed, perhaps you feel that opportunities are not available to you. What's stopping you from opening the gate and being more receptive to new opportunities or relationships?

Gifts

What gifts or talents should you embrace? Perhaps you are the giver of the gift and you feel that you have something to offer. Is it well received? If you are the recipient, accept the gift unconditionally. Being unappreciative could highlight your attitude to something in your life you ought to be more accepting of.

Hands see also Body

Hands are often seen in dreams, as they have a deeper significance than most other parts of the body. They are universal symbols of activity, generosity, productivity, creativity, an open heart and spirituality (praying hands). We also associate hands with communication – waving, cheering, raised hand for question, aggressive gestures, shaking hands for greeting and more. Many cultures use their hand gestures to enhance their communication skills. If you dream of any problem or injury to the hand it is a sign that you are feeling a lack of control or unable to perform your regular role.

House

If you are involved in moving or selling a house or simply have wanted to move, the dream will guide you to what you'd ideally love to live in – without the practicalities of price and location. Take note of how the house feels for you in the dream, rather than simply focusing on the actual design. Those characteristics may help you find your ideal house and location.

Generally, the house in a dream is a metaphor for the self and how you feel about yourself and your life. Each room represents different parts of you. Dreaming about a house will convey a great deal about your physical, emotional and personal life. Where is the house located? Is it in good condition or is it in need of repair? What parts of yourself are you neglecting? Where do you fit in? Do you feel happy and secure there? What is the view from the windows? All these details give you clues about where you are in your life and how you are feeling.

If you dream of previous homes or your childhood home, you're not necessarily longing or living for the past. What experiences did you have in the house and how did they become a framework for early behaviour patterns and belief systems? When we dream of our childhood home, our psyche is revisiting emotional issues in waking life that have to do with family values or domestic-related beliefs and how they were formed from those early years. If any of the rooms are cluttered or cramped with ornaments or the furniture covered in dust, explore the deeper metaphoric meanings.

Have you taken on too much responsibility and neglected your needs? Is it time to dust off your old ambitions or interests you put aside long ago? Are there old hurts you need to clean up so that you can feel refreshed and ready to start a new life again?

Attic

Attics are where we keep memorabilia, and therefore it's where our memories are stored away. As it's the highest room of the house (the dreamer's mind) it may suggest that you are exploring your higher self or a spiritual awakening. Looking for 'old clothing' would represent looking for old aspects or past experiences in your life.

Basement/cellar

The basement or the cellar is the subconscious/unconscious mind and all that is hidden away from plain sight, including your greatest fears and repressed parts of your personality. We also store what we don't need in the basement and what is usually not of immediate use, such as our undeveloped selves. It can be seen as psychological space where things are filed away for potential use.

Kitchen/dining room

The kitchen and dining room are where we are nourished and socialise with friends and family. It represents our social nature and it's the place we go to for comfort and relaxation. If there is conflict in a domestic situation, this is the place where it happens – at the hub or 'hearth' (emotional heart) of the home. It's also our place of creativity where we put together ingredients to create recipes and make delicious meals to our taste.

Bedroom

The bedroom is a place of intimacy, relationships and sleep (our unconscious minds). It is where we dress to suit the roles we play and so it can represent aspects of our persona. We use our bed to rest and recover, and it is therefore a refuge where we feel safe and relaxed.

Bathroom/toilet

The bathroom is our most private room in the house where we take care of our bodies – we cleanse, relax, pamper and make ourselves attractive. It's also a place of releasing and disposing of our bodily functions and so if there is a problem with the bathroom/toilet in your dream, it would indicate that you are not processing your feelings or are not having time out for yourself. Being unable to find a toilet or not having privacy highlights your embarrassment and vulnerability, and you may be finding it difficult to express your needs around some real-life issues.

Stairs

Stairs, like mountains, require climbing and symbolise the effort it takes to achieve your goals. They can also represent striving for increasing spiritual growth.

Secret Rooms

Dreaming of a secret room you never knew existed or one that has been rediscovered after being long forgotten is a symbol of our neglected potential. Our subconscious mind is trying to alert us to the fact that it's never too late to find those parts of yourself you've left behind or discarded.

This secret room has come into your dreams to remind you of your old hopes and aspirations – it may be that you're now in a new life transition and you can start dancing lessons you'd put off or go back to playing tennis that you enjoyed so much. Perhaps you're changing jobs or retired and would like to explore options that once held great interest for you.

If the secret room is in a dark area of the house and you're feeling terrified at entering it as it's locked or it's forbidden to enter (like Bluebeard's locked doors), it suggests our psyche is afraid of having to face hurtful memories of the past. It may contain repressed and unpleasant memories of events that you haven't fully dealt with or want to revisit.

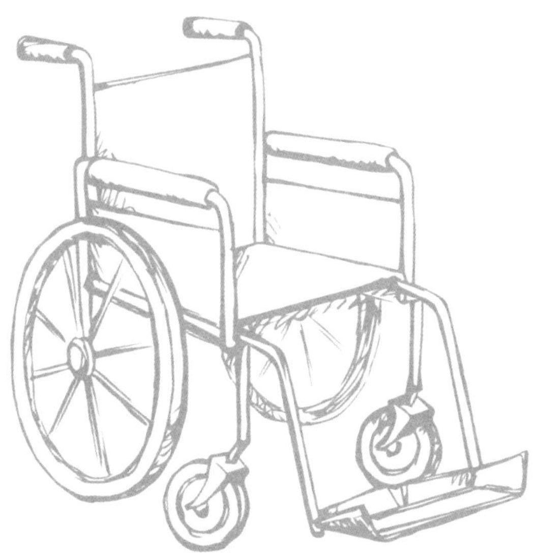

I

ILLNESS/INJURY see also Death/Dead

Dreams of being ill often represent periods when we are feeling depressed and our health and spiritual strength are not in top form. We talk of 'ailments' when describing symptoms of illness. Ask yourself what's ailing or troubling you. Dis-ease (disease) means not being at ease with your body. Take note from your dream scenes and the body parts highlighted to uncover what is making you feel ill at ease in your waking life. If you dream of a child being ill, it's more likely to do with emotional injury than physical. However, do monitor your health or your child's health, as our dreams can sometimes warn of health issues before they are diagnosed.

WATCH
2

J

JEWELLERY/VALUABLES see also Loss and Treasure

Jewellery represents qualities in us that we consider worthwhile, and how we are valued by others. Therefore, it's about self-image and personal value. Dreaming of jewellery points to what you hold to be of value and importance. A particular piece of jewellery may have a personal meaning for you in regards to an element/facet in your relationship. To dream of a jewellery box (your self-worth) symbolises how you see yourself, your values and potential. It's all contained within you.

If you can't find your jewellery, it indicates that you've neglected or repressed valuable parts of yourself. What is making you feel undervalued?

If the jewellery has a personal meaning for you in real life, it may be pointing you to those aspects of your life that need to be visited. To search for jewels is to search for your true self. To find jewels means you've uncovered latent valuable parts of yourself.

Jewels have always been regarded by the ancients as having powerful, magical and protective properties. A jewel in the crown shows that you have achieved recognition and self-awareness. Look at your personal association with each jewellery piece.

K

Keys

Are you trying to find a solution to your problem? If the key won't open the lock, it means you need to find alternatives and it's best to ask for advice. Key is synonymous with locking and unlocking. Have you been keeping your emotions and feelings all locked up? 'My lips are sealed' is also an idiom meaning discretion and being able to keep matters confidential. In a nightmare, we lose our keys, the door won't open or we fumble. These scenarios reflect our real-life anxieties, fears and obstacles that we are trying to escape from. Keys and doorways often appear in our dreams when there are unexpected changes in our lives.

Kidnapping

Kidnapping suggests feeling that you have no control or you are dependent on someone for your well-being. Are you concerned about new and unexpected changes in your life? Is something valuable (a relationship, job, health) at risk of being taken away from you? You may well be feeling that you are being held at ransom and therefore have to compromise your ethics in some way. It is worth noting who the kidnapper is and what their terms are to give you clues into what's really going on at a conscious level.

Kiss see also Sex

Kiss suggests desire for romance, intimacy and the need to be close. It is also a symbol of acceptance or coming to terms with someone or something. Do you need to kiss and make up? It may be time to let go of someone/something and move on to a new stage in your life. The emotions connected to the kiss in the dream hold the key to the best possible meaning.

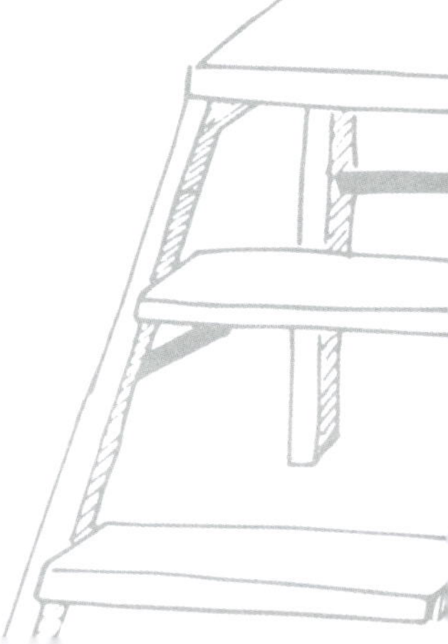

L

Ladders

Ladders in dreams are all about direction in the dreamer's life. If you are climbing up it suggests you are reaching out for new opportunities, and making progress. If there are obstacles as you are climbing, consider what is stopping you from climbing your way to the top. Are you afraid to climb the social or corporate ladder? Are you under pressure to do so?

Do you want to climb beyond the last rung of the ladder and reach out for a spiritual awakening? Do you feel in your dream that the ladder is a stairway to heaven? Climbing down the ladder or falling off has more of a negative connection to failure, loss of ambition, status and loss of control, as in 'downward spiral'.

Loss

If you dream of losing possessions, such money, keys, wallet, pets, car, jewellery or children, it suggests that these things are of value to you and their loss indicates that you are afraid of facing financial loss or loss of status in your daily life. What would it mean to lose your worth (money), ID (wallet), car/home (keys), relationships (children, pets)? These fears and anxieties reflect how you are feeling in your waking life. The dream may be asking you to look at what you may potentially lose, and appreciate and value those things that you have. It may additionally be showing you that you are in danger of losing elements that you value unless you change your attitude and habits.

M

Machines

Often machinery in dreams represents how our body and our lifestyle are functioning. Are you an automated machine? Do you need to leave your monotonous job? Perhaps your robotic lifestyle is in need of a makeover?

If the machine malfunctions, it indicates that you may be experiencing a few disappointments and setbacks in your waking life. Problems with machines such as televisions or computers suggest difficulty in processing or accessing information. You may also be spending too much time online and losing communication skills and connection with people you know or could potentially come to know.

Money

We would like to believe that dreaming of money means that money is coming to us in real life. Although this is mostly considered to be a wish fulfilment dream, sometimes this type of dream can be showing us what is possible to gain as a reward for our efforts, or simply that we'll win the lottery or at the races. Unfortunately, there is a relatively small chance of this dream coming true.

Money in dreams is more than a representation of wealth, success and power. It also relates to self-worth and an exchange of value. What is valuable to us cannot always be paid for in money. Time, health, love and well-being are worth a great deal. Lack of money or losing money is alerting you to the 'cost' of losing something that means a great deal to you. What's costing you at the moment? Perhaps the dream is asking you to redefine or reassess your values.

Banknotes represent power and your potential for success or your actual financial situation. It may also symbolise your creative and emotional life. You're rich in talent and in your relationship. If you are giving money away it may be expressing your goodwill to help others in financial troubles or you may be simply giving them the richness of your wisdom and advice.

Mountains

If you dream of successfully climbing a mountain in your dream, it indicates that you have overcome obstacles and reached your goal. A slippery slope suggests that you are feeling insecure as you face struggles at home or at work. Dreaming of climbing a mountain is a metaphor for encountering obstacles in your waking life and the ability to keep going until you reach the summit. If you are afraid of heights, it may suggest that you are not ready for success or that you fear failure (slipping down). Do you have a mountain of work you cannot get under control?

Mountains are also known as mystical places and therefore can represent our spiritual journey to reach a higher level of consciousnesses. To look out from the top of a mountain is to review your life.

N

Naked

To dream of being naked is to feel vulnerable and exposed in your day-to-day life. Nudity is a symbol of revealing our true (original) selves to others, unable to hide behind the safety of our clothing. Being comfortable naked means 'what you see is what you get' and that you are being honest and genuine in your approach to a situation with nothing to hide.

Numbers

Numbers hold a different significance for each of us. A number can refer to age, amounts of things, dates, time, address, and other associations that are relevant to you. These numbers are regarded as universal symbols with the most common associations; however, treat numbers in dreams as codes that are unique to you. Taking a numerology approach: if you dream of a number with more than one digit you may wish to add them to a single digit. For example, 24 can be reduced to 6 (2+4=6).

1. Number one is the beginning and end of all things, the source, wholeness, unity, individuality, self. Check in with yourself and make sure you are balanced and have not spread yourself too thinly.
2. Duality (yin/yang, yes/no, good/bad) balance, choice and relationships. Look at the choices you are making. Are you procrastinating? Do your relationships need work?
3. Creative power. Middle, beginning and ending. The family unit of mother, father, child. Do you feel complete? Are you ready for something new? It may be time to complete that creative project.
4. Balance, life cycle, four seasons, earth, nature elements. Is your 'house' in order? Is your life stable? Look at what needs to be structured.
5. Represents the human body with its five fingers, toes and senses. It's also about movement and motion. Are you stuck? Do you need to move or travel to get away?
6. Balance, harmony and health are the characteristics of this number. Are you living in the moment? Are you spending time with people you love or are you out of balance?
7. This mystical number is associated with victory, magic and healing. Other symbolic meanings include seven days a week, seven stages of man, seven colours of rainbow and seven chakras. Everything goes in

cycles – what is coming up for you now? Look at developing new skills and be ready for new insights.

8. The symbol of the number 8 on its side means infinity and so it suggests regeneration, new achievements and higher consciousness. What new lifestyle changes are coming your way?
9. The number of completion of a cycle before a new one begins (pregnancy and childbirth). You are on the verge of a new adventure – the last number before you complete your cycle. Do you need to go back to your roots before you move forward to your next phase?
10. The law of heaven and earth, Ten Commandments, balance and unity. If you add 1 and 0 it will give you 1. Is it time for a new beginning?
11. In numerology, 11 is a master number – that is, it is not added up to make a single digit. In dreams, the number 11 stands for mastery, spirituality and intuition. Do you have a vision of the kind of life you wish to create?
12. Symbol of cycles and cosmic order. There are 12 signs of the zodiac, 12 disciples of Christ, 12 months of the year. What cycle are you part of right now?

O

OCEAN see Water

OWL see Animals – Birds

P

PARALYSIS/BEING PARALYSED see also Trapped

In your dream you try to move but your legs won't carry you. You're paralysed. Stuck. You begin to speak but no words come out or they're all jumbled and you choke. This is a common dream, which is often referred to as a nightmare because of the lack of control/powerlessness and impending threat as a result of someone chasing you or inability to cry out for help.

A paralysis dream suggests that you feel that you are not making progress in waking life and that something is holding you back, preventing you from achieving your goal. It may well be self-sabotage – which is why you are making such a great effort to move but are getting nowhere – you're stuck in a rut. Paralysis in a dream is also an indication of natural paralysis when the body needs to remain still during REM sleep.

PARTY/CELEBRATIONS see also Wedding

Dreaming of parties and celebrations can indicate the anxiety you experience around these events. Celebrations are positive experiences, celebrating joyful occasions; however, if you are not feeling happiness in your dream, it suggests that you are not feeling at ease in a social environment. It may also mean that you wish to experience joy or that the celebration is coming your way soon. Do you need to celebrate something in your life, no matter how insignificant it may appear to others?

Christmas, New Year and other major ritual celebrations and festivals are usually stressful times when expectations and hype are experienced. What do the events/celebrations mean to you personally and how do they relate to your real-life expectations of others and yourself? Note the emotion in your dream. Ritual celebrations have a specific message – baptism is for beginnings and belonging; graduation is indicative of opportunities and success.

Dreaming of weddings is the most common celebration dream. At a symbolic level, it is about commitment and relationships. Are you ready to go into a partnership or relationship? Your old identity has to merge with the new person, which requires a loss of old identity, and so there may be a sad emotion associated with weddings. It's common to have a death dream at the same time as a wedding dream.

People

People in our dreams illustrate aspects of our relationships to others and with ourselves. Archetypal characters are universal as they represent types of people we meet and qualities we possess and those same qualities we associate with others. When dreaming of people, work out what each person represents to you. Use three words to describe each person in your dream and then ask yourself if these characteristics have been evident in your life recently or if perhaps you could benefit from incorporating them.

Mother

The mother figure is an important archetypal figure in our dreams, representing both the nurturing, protective aspects and the possessive, domineering sides of ourselves. Mother is a symbol of the earth – Mother Nature – and all those qualities associated with growth, fertility, fragility and nurturing. Do you need these qualities in your life? Are you over-nurturing others and need more self-care? Perhaps you need to integrate the positive and negative aspects of the mothering role for a more balanced outcome.

Father see also Authority Figures below

The father in your dream commonly represents an authoritarian figure. You may have authoritarian qualities within you that need addressing or perhaps these qualities have dominated your life and you no longer wish to be treated in a paternalistic manner. Other common figures that are associated with authority, power, masculinity and wisdom come in dreams as a king, judge, priest, boss, police or old man. Are you struggling with authority or do you feel inadequate in an area of your life? Your association with your own father or father figure is the key to working out the dream's message.

Stranger

Dreaming of a stranger represents those aspects of yourself that you haven't met yet and may be a little bit tentative to explore. If you are a tourist in your dream, it suggests that you look at something in your life from a new perspective.

Authority figures

Authority figures such as fathers, teachers, police, judges, bosses or priests represent the qualities that are unique to their role. It is possible that these qualities can be used in your current situation. Perhaps they bring up negative emotions from the past at a time when you considered yourself powerless as a dependent. The teacher is a symbol of learning and knowledge – perhaps this is an area which you need to explore in more detail in your waking life. Police and judges are part of the legal system and therefore are law enforcers. What do their characteristics mean to you personally? Dreaming of your boss is a common dream, as it reflects your real-life conflict with authority. Each of these figures could be replacing anyone with authority in your life.

Plane

Are you going on a big journey or heading off in a new direction? Planes involve long and quick travel, and represent our path and aspirations in life. A smooth flight signals that you are comfortable with this, while a turbulent one is preparing you for bumps along the way. Flying is also about desire for freedom, wild sexual abandonment and escape. If you have trouble packing your bags, are getting on the wrong plane, are missing the plane or are simply not being able to take off, consider what obstacles and anxieties are preventing you from reaching your ideal goal.

Are you prepared for the new venture? Dreaming of a plane crash may mean that there are changes ahead out of your control.

PREGNANCY see also Babies

Pregnancy is the creation of life that we associate with creativity. Are you dreaming of being more creative or are you contemplating starting a new project? A man who dreams of being pregnant may be in a situation where his creativity is being questioned or rejected. Usually in dreams, men give birth to an object rather than a baby – one that is relevant to what they aim to achieve.

If you dream of being pregnant, it suggests the birth of something new – a new idea, project, lifestyle. Someone else being pregnant indicates that something is not being expressed in you.

R

Rescue

If you dream of being rescued, the dream could be telling you that you need rescuing – possibly from yourself or from a situation that you are not in control of. What do you need to be rescued from? If there is water in your dream, it symbolises your emotional life and therefore is related more to a relationship issue. If you are the rescuer, the dream highlights your desire to be noble and heroic and a need for validation. Examine the dream and notice who or what you are rescuing.

Roads

Roads are symbols of our life direction and spiritual journey. We talk about our life's journey or the path we are on and being at a crossroad when we need to make a decision. Looking at the road behind you is to look back at your past; looking ahead is your future. What kind of road are you travelling on? If it's a rocky road, you may have some obstacles facing you; a side track or unpaved road suggests that you may go off track or that it will be more rewarding to have reached your destination in your own way.

Streets also suggest navigation – you may need to check in or stop and get directions along the way to help you in your present journey. Consider the following associations with roads for further insight: road rage, on the road, one for the road, on the road to recovery, all roads lead to Rome.

S

School

School, college or other educational institutions epitomise learning, and if you are having recurring dreams of being back in school, it often reflects performance anxiety in your waking life. Are you keeping up your grades? Do you need to retrain or upskill? The more advanced the level of education, the more complex the information and more pressure for you to perform in real life. It may be time to implement some changes to do with knowledge and learning.

Searching

To search for something often denotes a need to know and understand yourself. What you are searching for in the dream will give you a deeper insight into what those images represent for you. For example, searching for a child may indicate the need to find the inner child within you or if it's your child, you associate the child with something of utmost value.

Sex

Freud saw sex as wish fulfilment, but his theory has been disputed by many working in the area of dreams. Dreaming of sex has physical and emotional interpretations. For men, a wet dream is a biological function that involuntary releases semen while they are asleep, usually triggered by a sex dream. For women, they can also experience sexual stimulation and pleasure in their dreams – our bodies crave for a physical release. There is research on hormonal and physical changes, and the higher levels of oestrogen that produce more sex dreams. Circumstances surrounding the experience of a sex dream can vary from pleasurable to disturbing and distressing.

Symbolically, sexual intercourse indicates a desire for emotional bonding, closeness and intimacy. It is a longing for a deeper communication on a more intimate level that connects you to someone else.

Sex with others

Often sex functions as a metaphor for being attracted to qualities that your dream sexual partner represents. Sex with an older person suggests you are looking for nurturing, stability, compassion, wisdom and security. If you dream of having sex with a celebrity, it indicates you wish to have those same qualities of fame and recognition in your life. Sex with someone you work with is a representation of a good working relationship.

Having sex with a stranger or someone you are not attracted to means you are coming across something in your life that you are not consciously aware of, such as emotional connections, closeness, and deep emotions associated with intimacy. These qualities may be missing from your life or conversely, you don't want emotional involvement that requires commitment to complicate your life.

Sex with your ex

Having sex with your ex is not about wanting to act on the desire or even having those feelings for your ex in real life. Usually it represents our previous experience with past romantic relationships and wanting to recapture the 'best' of that experience to integrate into your present relationship. What do you need to feel more loving?

Storms

Stormy weather is an indicator of the level of turmoil in your emotional life and powerful changes, depending on how dramatic the weather is. Extreme natural events such as cyclones, tornadoes, hurricanes and tsunamis are signs of sudden and unexpected changes in your life and their effect on you. What strong emotions are surging through you?

The havoc and devastation they wreak suggest that you are feeling out of control in your waking life. Perhaps an escape plan can be devised so that you emerge with as little damage as possible. There is wisdom to be gained after one of these stormy dreams.

T

Trapped/Stuck

This dream usually manifests as a nightmare and it represents our inability to escape something in real life and being unable to see a way out of the situation. You may be stuck in a job you don't like or feel trapped in a relationship that is no longer fulfilling. If you are setting a trap or falling into a trap in your dreams, take note of the dream scene as it may give you insight into what or who you are trying to hold on to. Perhaps the dream is warning you not to get caught in a trap.

Treasure

To dream that you found treasure suggests that you have discovered a hidden talent or skill that you did not know you possessed. You will also be helped by a lot of people, which will allow you to achieve your goals.

Trees

Dreaming of a tree can symbolise a tree of life, a family tree or the tree of knowledge. It can represent characteristics associated with the symbol, depending on your beliefs and customs. Trees represent our life force and trees are also known as the lungs of the planet. Dreaming of a tree is highlighting your developmental growth and connections to your family 'roots', which hold you in the solid earth as foundations. If the tree is swaying, it indicates that your family or foundations are not as solid as they should be. Branching out suggests new direction, and buds and fruits are different stages of our life. If you are alighting from a branch, you may be feeling out on a limb. Is it a majestic oak tree or a spiny yucca? What characteristics do you associate with these trees? The type of tree and its overall appearance is important to note in the dream so that you can assess its significance in your daily life.

V

VEHICLES see also Car

Our vehicles show direction, power, navigation and innovations. They are totally reliant on humans to create and operate them, and therefore are associated with our ambition, purposefulness and willpower. Each vehicle is built for a purpose and therefore the dream will highlight your needs and wants. For example, a truck is to carry goods – it may suggest that you are carrying a heavy load (burden), or an ambulance indicates a health emergency. Are you taking care of your health needs? Vehicles also give us an option to travel and escape. Trains and buses can be for necessary trips into work but can also offer long distance journeys at a moderate pace where one can enjoy the scenery. Train tracks are directional and therefore a metaphor for our journey and direction in life – both inner and outer journeys. Do you need to escape from the daily grind and find a new direction in your life.

Volcano

Dreaming of a volcano represents the rising emotional pressure that is ready to erupt in a violent outburst. There may be someone in your waking life that you feel has an explosive personality or your home/work life is like a volcano waiting to erupt. Perhaps it could be that you're suppressing anger and you may need to let off steam in a way that is not destructive.

Water

Water is a powerful symbol of the collective unconscious as it is lifegiving to all living things. Water is life. Water cleanses and purifies and is often seen as a sign of rebirth, spirituality and healing. Many Hindus believe that the water from the Ganges River can cleanse a person's soul of all past sins, and that it can also cure the ill.

We refer to water as a body of water, and our human body is made up of over seventy per cent of water. It is not surprising that water is a powerful symbol in dreams, and we collectively dream of floods, tidal waves, ocean, seas, lakes and ponds. How you are feeling in real life or emotions you are repressing in your life will appear in dreams as water themes. Is everything smooth sailing at home or are you being tossed about and afraid of drowning? One dream image suggests you are in control of your emotional life and the other indicates feeling overwhelmed and literally 'adrift'. The type of vessel you are on suggests the resources you have in dealing with your emotions. A large cruise ship will withstand the pounding of the waves better than an unsteady raft or a leaky canoe. You may need to take a closer look at your support systems.

If the water is muddy or the waves are pounding and you are afraid of drowning, it represents those swelling feelings associated with feeling swamped during a significantly stressful and confusing period in your life. If you can breathe underwater, you will have faced your deepest emotions without drowning in them. Clear waters symbolise clarity – you will see your way through.

Oceans and seas suggest the vastness and depths of our psyche and our soul. How you navigate or swim in these large bodies of water and their depths will give you insight into your deepest emotions.

Pools, dams and ponds are more contained, suggesting you don't like to delve too deeply in your emotional state.

Flowing water means movement and change, while stagnant and dirty water, such as swamps, suggests you are stuck or confused. A waterfall is about releasing strong emotions.

Falling in the water suggests that you are not ready emotionally for whatever is going on in your life. You need to get rid of all the past clutter and belief patterns first.

Drowning, big waves, tsunami, tidal waves or flooding represent your feelings of being overwhelmed. Are you in denial of the emotional stress you are facing? Are there ways to better accept these feelings that often involve vulnerability and lack of control? If you dive under the tidal wave and don't run from it, it suggests that you are willing to meet challenges in your life.

Weather see also Storms

Weather symbolises powerful emotions and change. It's important to understand what stage we are in our own journey through life. In all seasonal/weather cycles there is always a rebirth after death (winter to spring). Rain represents both an emotional release and replenishment for the earth (potential growth). When it's sunny in our dreams, all is well and full of optimism ahead. Snow can indicate an emotional coldness and that you may need to thaw out a little. Fog represents a lack of clarity ahead, so it's best to move slowly and with caution when making decisions. Wind is a symbol of change and the idiom 'wind of change' reflects its nature.

Wedding see also Party/Celebrations

Women are more likely than men to dream about weddings and the dream scenes tend to have more negative components than positive ones.

It may be that the bride goes to the wrong church, is late or can't get there, or it's the wrong groom. These anxiety dreams are not necessarily related to women who are in committed relationships or about to get married.

Generally, wedding dreams represent commitment and the beginning of a new partnership. If you see yourself as the bride or groom and you are happy, it indicates that you want to be more involved in your current relationship. It may suggest that you are searching for an inner marriage – an integration of the yin and yang, the feminine and the masculine, the Anima and Animus. The marriage in your dream may represent the union of the different sides of your own character.

If your biological time clock is ticking away and you are anxious to get married, this dream may be a form of wish-fulfilment. In some cultures, wedding dreams are interpreted as possible deaths of someone you know. This is true in a way, as women who take on their husband's name have to 'kill' their old identity and reinvent themselves with a new name that requires tedious bureaucratic processes. Marriage is the death of the old life and the birth of a new one and it is common to have a death dream and a wedding dream in sequence.

About the author

Rose Inserra is a successful published author of over sixty books distributed both here and internationally. She has been listed in the Notable Books in the Children's Book Council Awards and short-listed for the Environment Award for Children's Literature in Australia.

Her best-selling book, *Dictionary of Dreams*, has sold more than half-a-million copies and has become a trusted and practical source for people who wish to gain insight into their dreams. Rose also regularly assists people with interpreting their dreams via private consultations, group sessions and seminars, which have resulted in major life-changing moments for them. She is a member of the International Association for the Study of Dreams and has appeared as a guest columnist and speaker in print media and on radio.

For more information, visit www.roseinserra.com

More titles in the series ...

The Gift of Flowers

ISBN 978-1-925429-97-8

The Gift of Spells

ISBN 978-1-925429-37-4

The Gift of Crystals

ISBN 978-1-925017-82-3

The Gift of Nature

ISBN 978-1-925682-27-4

Available at all good bookstores